World's Most Mysterious
"TRUE" GHOST STORIES

Ron Edwards
Illustrated by Jim Sharpe

Sterling Publishing Co., Inc.   New York

For Kristine Mae

Library of Congress Cataloging-in-Publication Data

Edwards, Ron, 1930–
    World's most mysterious "true" ghost stories / by Ron Edwards ;
illustrated by Jim Sharpe.
        p.   cm.
    Includes index.
    Summary: A collection of thirty-one brief, true tales of
unexplained disappearances, haunting ghosts, and other phenomena.
    ISBN 0-8069-3872-2
    1. Ghosts—Juvenile literature. [1. Ghosts.] I. Sharpe, Jim.
ill.   II. Title.
BF1461.E38   1996
133.1—dc20   95-46304
                                                      CIP
                                                       AC

10   9   8   7   6   5   4   3   2   1

Published by Sterling Publishing Company, Inc.
387 Park Avenue South, New York, N.Y. 10016
© 1996 by Ron Edwards
Illustrations © 1996 by Jim Sharpe
Distributed in Canada by Sterling Publishing
℅ Canadian Manda Group, One Atlantic Avenue, Suite 105
Toronto, Ontario, Canada M6K 3E7
Distributed in Great Britain and Europe by Cassell PLC
Wellington House, 125 Strand, London WC2R 0BB, England
Distributed in Australia by Capricorn Link (Australia) Pty Ltd.
P.O. Box 6651, Baulkham Hills, Business Centre, NSW 2153, Australia
Manufactured in the United States of America
All rights reserved

Sterling ISBN 0-8069-3872-2

CONTENTS

1. JOURNEYS THROUGH TIME

"The most beautiful thing we can experience is the mysterious."
—Albert Einstein

Yesterday Is Today

On July 14, 1944, Royal Air Force pilot Thomas Clifford strafed a column of German tanks that were on their way to hammer Allied positions in Normandy. After several attacks, the 23-year-old squadron leader banked his Typhoon fighter away from the burning wreckage and headed back to his base.

North of Amiens, he spotted two planes that seemed to be engaged in a dogfight. As he flew closer, he identified one as an ancient SE5 biplane, used by the British during World War One. The pilot was in trouble, trying to control the plane as smoke streamed from the damaged engine.

Then Clifford noticed the plane that had attacked the

SE5, and was astonished to see that it too was from World War One, a Luftwaffe triplane with large black Maltese crosses on the wings and fuselage.

He watched the German fighter close in on the SE5 for the kill and decided to participate. Clifford fired one burst from his guns and the tracers sliced into the archaic Fokker, but seemed to have no effect.

As the Fokker dived for safety in the clouds below, the young squadron leader noticed a look of fear on the German pilot's face.

The British SE5 was still struggling to remain airborne, but the pilot waved from his open cockpit and rocked his wings in gratitude. Clifford returned the wave and watched the old warbird glide down to an emergency landing.

Upon returning to his base at Kent, Thomas Clifford reported damaging the German tank convoy and casually mentioned that he had also taken a few shots at an antique German Fokker. The report was filed and forgotten, and Clifford did not think about the encounter again until July 1972. The Royal Air Force was holding a reunion and Clifford was invited, along with other former officers who had fought in World War Two.

At the party in London, Clifford was introduced to retired Squadron Leader George Campbell, a former pilot with the Royal Flying Corps. Clifford was honored to meet with the old warrior who had earned the Distinguished Flying Cross during World War One.

As always happens at military reunions, the men exchanged war stories, and Clifford described the two obsolete combat planes he had met near Amiens while flying back to his base.

"The Germans were really desperate by 1944," Clifford said, "because they were using old Fokker triplanes for trainers. But that's not the only odd thing. The Fokker was actually attacking another old World War One plane I'm sure was a British SE5."

Most of the listeners dismissed the story with a wry smile, but George Campbell's face turned pale.

"Do you remember the date?" asked Campbell, after recovering his composure.

"Not after all these years," confessed Clifford. "But it must have happened in July. I remember that because my birthday is in July."

George Campbell stared at Clifford with tears in his eyes. "It was July 14, 1918. I was flying that SE5."

Now it was Clifford's turn to feel weak in the knees, as Campbell told him he had been on combat patrol near Amiens when bullets from an enemy plane struck his engine. The attacker was a blue and white Fokker DR-1 with three wings.

"I realized that the enemy pilot had the advantage," said Campbell, "and I was helpless as he came from behind to finish me off. Suddenly, I saw a strange aircraft diving and firing at the Fokker. The German quickly broke off his attack and headed for the clouds below us."

Icy fingers were crawling up Clifford's back as he listened to Campbell's story. He raised his hand and said, "I can tell you what happened next. Your engine was on fire and you waved to the strange airplane as you went down."

"That's right," exclaimed Campbell. "I was able to land but found myself on the wrong side of the lines. I was captured and put in a POW camp."

George Campbell told his listeners about a visitor he had while he was a prisoner of war. It was the pilot who had downed his SE5, a German ace who talked about attacking Campbell's plane, and wondered about the unfamiliar monoplane they had seen come out of no-where. The ace told Campbell he was glad the end of the war was near, because "that airplane could blow both of us out of the sky."

Campbell's visitor was Lieutenant Hermann Goering, holder of the Blue Max. He had assumed command of Captain Manfred von Richthofen's squadron after the Red Baron was shot down on April 21.

"It's very strange," said Tom Clifford, as he reminisced about his unusual experience. "I guess I could have flown into a time warp that day and slipped twenty-six years into the past. Campbell was convinced that I saved his life by firing at the old Fokker."

Lost in Time

Late one night in 1933, Father Litvinov was closing up the church and anticipating a peaceful sleep after a long, tiring day.

Just before midnight he heard the sound of frantic knocking. Father Litvinov opened the door to a young man dressed in strange clothes.

The man was trembling. Father Litvinov calmed the stranger and asked his name.

"I am Dmitri Grishkov," said the obviously frightened, confused man. "I am supposed to be married today."

Grishkov said he had stopped at the cemetery on his way to church. While paying respects to a friend who had died a year earlier, he suddenly saw that friend standing next to him. Then Grishkov said his memory was blank until nightfall. He next remembered walking back to the village, but became uneasy because nothing looked familiar in the small Siberian town.

Suddenly, Grishkov leaped from his chair and ran out the door, shouting that he must find his family and the girl he was going to marry.

Father Litvinov hurried to the door and watched the desperate young man running and yelling, until he suddenly vanished in a grey mist.

Although it was very late, Father Litvinov began searching parish records in hopes of learning something more about his midnight visitor. The records revealed that a frantic youth had also been seen by two other priests and a school teacher at various times during the last two centuries.

As Father Litvinov continued searching the journal, his finger came to rest on the name of Dmitri Grishkov. A notation said that on his wedding day in 1746, Dmitri Grishkov had stopped to visit a friend's grave and then disappeared. Grishkov was never again seen by his family, friends, or fiancée.

Ten Minutes Late

On a calm, clear night in 1963, a National Airlines jetliner was cruising smoothly above the Atlantic Ocean. The crew aboard the Boeing 727 admired the sparkling lights on Florida's coastline ahead.

Shortly after contacting Miami Approach Control, the huge three-engine airliner disappeared. All attempts to contact the plane were in vain.

The astonished air controllers couldn't imagine what had happened when the blip representing the plane vanished from their radar screens.

Miami Approach Control queried the crews of other planes flying in the same area as National's B-727. No one had seen a bright fireball signifying an explosion, and no reports were heard from a plane in distress.

Everything seemed to be routine in the moonlit skies over the Atlantic.

Then, ten minutes after the Boeing 727 disappeared from radar, it suddenly reappeared! And it reappeared in exactly the same location where it had vanished!

Anxious air controllers made contact with the plane. "How are you doing out there?"

"Everything's fine," said the captain. "It's a beautiful night."

The crew obviously did not know they had been missing in time and space for ten minutes. The rest of the airliner's flight was normal. After landing at Miami International Airport, it taxied to the gate.

As the pilots shut down the engines, they were mildly surprised by the flashing lights of emergency vehicles approaching their plane. Officials began to question passengers as they came out the door.

"How do you feel?"

"Did you experience anything unusual during the flight?"

The unexpected inquisition from the excited mob of officials confused and upset many passengers. The flight had been smooth and enjoyable. The only thing weird in their minds was the silly questions from the crowd blocking their path to the gate.

When told that their plane had vanished from radar for ten minutes, the crew thought someone was playing a joke on them. Officials could not convince them they had ceased to exist during a ten-minute period of the flight, nor that the plane suddenly reappeared on radar at the exact position it had disappeared.

"No matter what you say, Captain," said the airline's

gate agent, "I'll need a deviation report because you were ten minutes late."

"That's nonsense," said the captain, looking at his watch. "What time do you have?"

That's when the pilots became believers.

The crew checked their watches with clocks on the ground. The time on all their watches, as well as the clocks in the cockpit, were exactly ten minutes slower than the actual time.

Where did the airliner go when it vanished from radar? Somehow, the plane managed to slip into another dimension for ten minutes, and no one aboard was ever aware of any change.

View of the Future

Victor Goddard was in serious trouble. The 37-year-old Royal Air Force pilot had been on a reconnaissance flight over Scotland. As he headed back to the air base, he flew into the heart of a vicious storm. While dodging broiling cumulus clouds, he was unable to see prominent landmarks. Soon he was lost.

It was 1934 and Goddard's Hawker Hart biplane did not have the sophisticated electronic navigational aids that would serve so well in the future. He caught brief glimpses of the mist-shrouded terrain while flying between cloud layers, but could not determine his position.

Somewhere ahead was Drem, an abandoned RAF airfield. If he could find it, he could calculate a new course home. Now, however, he was having difficulty just seeing through his rainswept goggles in the open cockpit plane. Goddard was worried that his fragile craft might be ripped to shreds by the violent winds that were tossing him around the sky like a toy kite.

When his instincts told him he was nearing the deserted airfield, an incredible thing happened.

"Suddenly," he said later, "the area was bathed in an ethereal light, as though the sun were shining on a midsummer day."

Goddard eased back on the power and slipped downwards around the towering clouds.

Then he saw it. Drem was just ahead.

As he approached the field, however, he wondered if he was in the right place. The airfield below was not deserted. It was alive with intense activity. As mechanics worked on a line of training planes, linemen were fuelling other planes on the concrete tarmac.

Descending to fifty feet, the anxious pilot watched a group of cadets and instructors walking towards rows of yellow airplanes, parked on the ramp outside the huge hangars.

Victor Goddard's head was swimming with questions as he surveyed the unexpected scene. Why were the planes painted yellow? All trainers for the Royal Air Force were silver. And when had Drem been reactivated?

Finally, Goddard recognized familiar landmarks in the area and turned his Hawker Hart to a course that would take him home.

When he landed, he told his story, but no one believed it. His fellow airmen felt he had experienced a hallucination after being tossed around by the thunderstorm.

Four years would pass before Goddard learned the truth of what happened during that afternoon flight.

In 1934, Drem *was* an abandoned airfield whose hangars had almost collapsed. The runways and ramp areas were scarred with jagged holes and weeds.

But in 1938, as the ominous threat of war with Germany became a reality, Drem was reopened and rebuilt to train young men as fighter pilots. At that time, the color of the planes was changed from silver to yellow.

Goddard believed that when he descended below the clouds that stormy day in 1934, he slipped through a hole in time and flew four years into the future.

A Switch in Time

On a cloudy summer evening Bill Johnstone and Ian Lacey were enjoying a bicycle ride through the Welsh hills. Near Cynon Gap, a heavy rainstorm forced them to seek shelter at a nearby railway signal box. They could not imagine the eerie adventure awaiting them. The date was July 15, 1945.

The two friends parked their bikes and hurried inside the small house, where they were welcomed by an aging signalman.

After removing their drenched capes, they warmed themselves near the glowing stove and watched the old man manipulate several switching levers.

Bill and Ian thought there was something odd about him. His uniform did not resemble any they had seen in recent years. As he went about his work, the signalman kept mumbling to himself, but the two friends could not understand his ramblings.

At 8:15 Bill and Ian heard a train approaching, but couldn't see it through the rainswept windows. As the train roared past the signal box, the old man quickly began moving switching levers.

What happened next took both friends by surprise. Above the sound of the furious winds, they heard the unmistakable screech of metal wheels on railroad tracks, followed by a horrendous crash, and the anguished screams of passengers.

Instantly, they rushed outside and ran towards the calamity, which was momentarily hidden from view. When they reached the end of the platform, they could not believe their eyes.

There was no disaster—no buckled, shattered railroad cars, no smoking, damaged engine, and no passengers. Nothing but an endless expanse of rusted rails and weeds that stretched into the distant hills.

As they walked back to the signal box, they noticed it was now dark and deserted. The door was broken, flapping like a flag in the wind. Inside, they found another shock. The small room was a maze of cobwebs, and the stove did not look as if it had held a fire for a long time. The dusty floor was covered with leaves and the switching levers were stiff from age.

Bill looked inside the stove and pulled out several newspapers that were nearly twenty years old.

The two friends rode their bikes to an inn about five miles from the mysterious signal box. There they learned that many villagers believed the old signal box was haunted by the ghost of Joshua Thomas, the man who was on duty when the 8:15 slammed into another train. Joshua had fallen asleep, and then thrown the wrong switch when he heard the approaching express train. He was fired, found guilty, and hanged himself.

In their hotel room, Bill and Ian read the yellowed newspapers where the tragic story unfolded just as described at the inn.

One newspaper was dated December 4, 1927, and the headline said: "Train Crash Horror—16 Die." Next they looked at another edition published after the official inquiry. It was dated July 12, 1928, and said: "Signalman Blamed For Rail Crash." The Board members held that Joshua Thomas was solely responsible for the catastrophe. The saga ended in the issue for July 16, with a report that "Signalman Joshua Thomas was found hanged yesterday. . . ."

The photo of Joshua in the newspaper revealed the same man who had welcomed them into the signal box during the storm.

Bill and Ian were never able to find a reason for their unusual encounter. They only knew that when they walked into the signal box that stormy summer night at Cynon Gap, they stepped eighteen years into the past.

2. BACK FROM ETERNITY

"Absence of evidence is not evidence of absence."
—Anonymous

Stopover in a Small Town

On the afternoon of February 1, 1963, Thomas P. Meehan completed arbitrating a case for the State Department of Employment Appeals Bureau in Eureka, California. At two o'clock the 38-year-old attorney began the drive to his home in Concord.

He never made it.

While cruising along Highway 101, he began to feel drowsy and stopped at Myers Flat. He called his wife and said he was not feeling well. She suggested he get a good night's rest at a motel and come home the following morning.

Meehan drove to Redway and took a room at the Forty Winks Motel at 5:00 p.m. He tried to call his wife to let her know where she could reach him, but the phones were out of order.

One hour later he was feeling worse. He drove to Garberville and checked in at the emergency room of the Southern Humboldt Community Hospital. At 6:45 he told the duty nurse that he felt as if he were dead. She went to summon a doctor, but Meehan was not in the waiting room when they returned.

At 7:00, while driving on Highway 101, along the Eel River, a couple from Myers Flat told a Highway Patrol officer they had just seen a car veer off the road and crash into the river.

An hour later Meehan was back at the Forty Winks Motel, talking to owner Chip Nunnemaker. At 9:00, as the attorney said goodnight and headed for his room, Nunnemaker noticed fresh mud on Meehan's shoes and on the cuffs of his trousers. At the door, Meehan turned around and said, "Do I look like I'm dead? I feel like I've died and the whole world died with me."

Harry Young, a motel employee, went to Meehan's room thirty minutes later to tell him the phones were still not working, due to a storm. Meehan had changed clothes and was now wearing a black suit.

At 10:45 the Highway Patrol located Meehan's car in the Eel River, its tail lights glowing faintly below the murky water.

The body of Thomas Meehan could not be found, but footprints were found leading up the embankment for about thirty feet. Beyond that point the footprints ended and the mushy terrain was undisturbed.

On February 20 Thomas Meehan's body was recovered from the Eel River, about sixteen miles from where his car went into the water. The coroner said Meehan had survived the crash, only to drown later.

Did the ghost of Thomas Meehan return to the Forty Winks Motel and talk with the owner an hour after crashing into the Eel River? It was during this time that Chip Nunnemaker saw mud on Meehan's shoes and pants. Did Harry Young see Meehan's apparition wearing a different suit at 9:30? Both men accepted Meehan as a living person.

Thomas Meehan never checked out of the motel, and no one saw him again until nineteen days later when his body was found floating in the Eel River.

Had Meehan climbed thirty feet up the wet embankment? If so, what happened to him at the point where his footprints ended? Is that when he died and his spirit began wandering back and forth between the real world and eternity?

A World of Her Own

Dorothy Jacobsen was an outstanding nurse, as well as an excellent teacher, on the staff at Ellis Hospital in Schenectady, New York. While on duty her performance was exemplary, but her social life was more like that of a department store mannequin. Away from the hospital she faced an endless collage of dark, lonely nights.

One evening as Dorothy sat in her secluded room, she could no longer endure the agonizing despair that had become her only companion, and took her own life.

For the grieving hospital staff, life went on and Dorothy was all but forgotten a few months later.

Forgotten, but not gone.

During the night shift a nurse was surprised to see her dead colleague standing inside an elevator when the doors slid open.

Later, one of Dorothy's former students saw her dead instructor's reflection in the elevator's shiny metal wall. She spun around, but found no one behind her.

Others have encountered the phantom nurse and some have smelled the aroma of flowers or perfume. All have felt the elevator grow cold whenever Dorothy appears.

No one can explain why Dorothy Jacobsen's spirit wants to join her former colleagues for endless rides on an elevator. Perhaps, in death, her restless spirit searches for the companionship she could not find in her lonely life.

The Ghost and Telly Savalas

Telly Savalas, who portrayed a tough New York detective named Theo Kojak during five seasons on television, had an eerie experience that haunted him for years.

It was the night he hitched a ride with a ghost.

"I was going home from a date, just after three o'clock in the morning on Long Island, and ran out of gas," said Savalas.

"While taking a shortcut to the freeway through a park, I heard someone say, 'I'll give you a lift.' I turned around and saw a man in a car. I hadn't even heard the car drive up, but there it was, so I got in and we drove to the gas station."

Savalas was embarrassed because he did not have enough money to buy gas. He offered to leave his watch as collateral, but the man in the car said, "I'll loan you a dollar."

"I took the dollar and asked him to write down his name and an address where I could repay him."

During the drive back from the service station, the man mentioned an unfamiliar name.

"Who is he?" asked Savalas.

"He plays baseball with the Red Sox."

The two men had not been discussing sports and Savalas thought the comment was rather strange.

Arriving at his car, Savalas thanked the man for his help, put the gas in the tank and drove home.

The next day, when Savalas bought a newspaper, one headline gave him cold chills. It announced the death of the ballplayer mentioned by the good samaritan who had given him a ride. Apparently, the young athlete had died at about 3:30 in the morning, the same time the man said he knew him.

Savalas later looked at the small slip of paper with a name and phone number in Boston. He dialed and a man answered, "Jimmy's Bar."

"Can I talk to Mr. Cullen, please?" asked Savalas. The line went silent, then he heard a woman's voice.

"Can I help you?" said the woman.

"I'd like to speak to Mr. James Cullen."

"He's not here."

"When do you expect him? He gave me a ride night before last and said I could reach him at this number."

"Is that right?" she said suspiciously. "What did he look like?"

Savalas thought he was getting the runaround, but gave her a description of the man and the clothes he was wearing. Suddenly, she started crying hysterically.

"I don't know what kind of a dirty trick you're trying to play on me," she screamed, "but Jim Cullen was my husband. He died three years ago!"

Savalas was shocked, but tried to calm the woman, explaining that he had no intention of hurting her; then he told her how he got the name and number.

When they met sometime later, Mrs. Cullen brought a letter her husband had sent while in the Army. The signature on the letter matched the one on the note. Savalas also learned that the suit Cullen wore during their ride was the same one in which he had been buried.

"I actually accept it as a phenomenon that I don't understand," admitted Savalas. "All I know is that I seemingly took a ride with a dead man."

The Lady on the Stairs

New Orleans is known for Mardi Gras festivals, delicious Creole cuisine, and Dixieland jazz. It also has the distinction of being the most haunted city in America. There are many opinions about which house is the most haunted, but one structure built in 1830 has an especially intriguing resident.

The two-and-a-half-storey house at 2606 Royal Street has French doors, a large fireplace, a winding stairway, and a beautiful Creole lady with long dark hair who glides down the stairs. The lovely woman, wearing a V-neck lace dress, died more than ninety years ago.

Some have seen the brown-eyed phantom in the rooms. One occupant, lying in bed one evening, thought he saw his wife standing at the door. Before he could speak, he felt movement in the bed and turned to see his wife beside him. Quickly, he looked across the room, but the image was gone.

While climbing the stairs, one man was forced to step aside and allow the dark-haired lady to pass. As she moved by, the terrified man felt an icy chill and rushed to his bedroom, quickly locking himself in.

One evening a woman heard the cries of her infant grandchild. Upon entering its room she was surprised to see a lovely woman in a lace dress bending over the crib. When the grandmother called out, the mysterious woman walked through a wall.

Unpleasant things have befallen some who have seen the strange vision. One young man was killed in an automobile accident right after meeting the lovely ghost on the stairs. Another man became so emotionally disturbed that he tried to commit suicide.

Some residents have heard the midnight moans of a woman crying in the attic, though that area of the house has been sealed off for years.

The apparition is believed to be the spirit of Madame Mineurecanal, a Creole lady who hanged herself over the staircase in the early 1900s.

3. RESTLESS SPIRITS

*"Absent in body,
but present in spirit."*
—I Corinthians. V.3

Spectre at the Helm

Captain Joshua Slocum was a nautical dreamer whose home became the oceans of the world. Slocum was born in Nova Scotia in 1844. While working as an apprentice bootmaker, he yearned to sail aboard the tall ships he admired from his window. Dreams became reality when he abandoned the bootshop and became a ship's cook.

As the years passed, Slocum worked his way up the ranks, sailing aboard large ships that took him to Africa, China, Australia, and the East Indies as well as exotic ports of call in the South Pacific.

Eventually, he received his master's license and commanded many vessels while logging thousands of miles across the seven seas.

Captain Slocum earned a unique place in maritime history when he became the first to sail a small boat alone around the world. His experience as a master navigator served him well for this journey, but he was not prepared for the eerie encounter he had with an unusual sailor during a three-year voyage aboard the *Spray.*

It happened while Slocum was sailing alone near the Azores. He became ill and was soon huddled in pain on the deck of his tiny cabin. A violent storm erupted, but he was too weak to go topside and trim the sails.

Hours later the gale was still raging as Slocum sat up and looked out the companionway. He felt uneasy and stared in confusion at the sight of a man at the helm, holding the *Spray* on a steady course.

The oddly dressed helmsman stared at Slocum and said: "I'm from Christopher Columbus' crew, and the pilot of the *Pinta.* I've come to guide your boat."

Slocum collapsed and slept through the night. When he awoke the next morning he felt better and the storm had abated. The mysterious helmsman was gone. Slocum could not decide if he had been dreaming, hallucinating, or had actually seen the ghostly image at the wheel.

The sails should have been ripped to shreds by the winds, yet they were intact and set. Slocum calculated that the thirty-six-foot yawl had travelled ninety miles, *on course,* throughout the stormy night. Only a skillful helmsman could have accomplished that incredible feat—even if he was from the 15th century.

A Patch of Fog

In the winter of 1918, Lieutenant David McConnel and
Lieutenant Larkin were two young pilots in the Royal
Flying Corps. On December 7 David McConnel was
scheduled to deliver a Sopwith Camel to Tadcaster, only
sixty miles away. He would be followed by another pilot
who would pick him up and return to their base.

Larkin was reading a newspaper when he heard his
roommate at the window.

"Hello," said Larkin. "I thought you were flying this
morning."

"I'm on my way now," McConnel said and grinned,
"but I forgot my map."

Larkin grabbed the chart from the desk and handed
it to his friend.

"Thanks," said McConnel. "Should be back by tea time," he added as he ran towards the flight line.

McConnel greeted the pilot who would bring him home in the two-seat Avro. They climbed into their planes, the engines came to life, and the two men were soon airborne.

En route they were forced to land because of heavy fog. McConnel went to a phone and called his base. The commander advised him to return now if he thought it was unsafe to continue. McConnel felt confident he could complete the flight.

They took off, but the swirling fog only got worse. When halfway to Tadcaster, McConnel saw the Avro pilot descend and make an emergency landing in a field. McConnel continued, certain that he could find a hole and land at his destination.

At 3:25 that afternoon, Larkin was reading a book when David McConnel came into the room. He was still wearing his flight suit and seemed happy to be back home.

"Hello, David," said Larkin. "How was the flight?"

"Ran into some fog, but got there all right," said McConnel. "Had a good trip." As he turned to go, he said, "Cheerio," and then walked out.

Later, another friend dropped in to tell Larkin that he and McConnel planned to dine at the Albion Hotel in Lincoln. Larkin said he would join them.

When Larkin arrived at the hotel, he got a drink and looked for McConnel. He walked across the room and joined a crowd of fellow officers near the fireplace. At a nearby table, he overheard a pilot discussing an accident involving a Sopwith Camel.

When Larkin heard "Tadcaster," he went to the table. "Excuse me," he said, "but I thought I heard you mention Tadcaster. My roommate, Dave McConnel, took a Camel there this morning."

"Yes," said the pilot. "It's really a shame. Poor chap. We just got the word at the base."

"What do you mean?" Larkin said curiously. "I saw him this afternoon. He was in a cheerful mood."

"I'm really sorry," said the pilot. His expression seemed apprehensive as he glanced around the table, then looked at Larkin. "I don't think you saw your friend this afternoon. McConnel crashed while trying to land in heavy fog. He was killed instantly."

Larkin learned details of the accident the next day from the operations officer. When McConnel's plane nose-dived into the runway at Tadcaster, his head smashed into the machine gun mount over the small windscreen.

David McConnel's wristwatch had stopped upon impact with the ground at 3:25—the precise time Larkin had seen him enter their room.

More Than Meets the Eye

The legendary *Queen Mary* is an elegant ship with a history of countless voyages between New York and England. Now a tourist attraction in Long Beach, California, she has exquisite cuisine, lavish stage extravaganzas, charming boutiques, and priceless art treasures.

She also has three ghosts.

The *Queen Mary*'s log documents the deaths of three people aboard the floating palace: a woman passenger, a crewman, and a cook.

In the 1950s, the woman passenger drowned after being pushed into the swimming pool. Her ghost is the one that is seen most often. Unsuspecting witnesses claim she is a woman in her forties, wearing a striped bathing suit. She appears at the indoor pool, walks towards the diving board, then disappears. Some have seen wet footprints leading away from the pool.

The other deaths occurred during World War Two. One involved a seaman who was crushed accidentally by a hatchway door. The cook's untimely demise was not an accident. He suffered a bizarre roasting when he was murdered by angry soldiers who pushed him into an oven. At the time, the *Queen Mary* was serving as an Army troop ship. Rumor has it that the combat infantrymen could no longer tolerate the cook's bland sustenance during the long voyage to England.

An executive with the company that manages the luxury liner admits, "There have been some strange things going on that cannot be explained by normal means."

Several employees have heard the sounds of a wild party in the pool area, only to find the place empty behind closed doors.

A security guard, walking a corridor with his watchdog, approached the hatch where the unfortunate seaman was crushed. Suddenly, the dog stopped and snarled, bared its teeth, and refused to move.

Other guards have had eerie experiences during their shifts. On G Deck they see lights going on and off and hear the sound of doors slamming. In locked areas, restricted to tourists, sensor alarms go off at night when no one is near them. Knocking noises, like pipes hammering, have been heard behind the walls, but the staff knows that no pipes are there.

A security guard was startled one night as she made her rounds. "I was going up the escalator when I felt like someone was staring at me. I turned and saw a man with a black beard, wearing dark blue coveralls. I stepped aside to let him pass, and he vanished!"

Although the world's largest cruise ship no longer makes trans-Atlantic crossings, the elegant lady still offers exciting adventures to those who walk up her gangplank. If you should ever tour the *Queen Mary,* remember that all the people you see may not be tourists. Somewhere along the way you may see a woman wearing a striped bathing suit, or a bearded man in dark blue coveralls, or . . .

"Don't Jump Again"

When Pauline Kane stepped aboard an airplane to go skydiving one afternoon, she could not know that her life would soon be changed by advice from a phantom.

The 26-year-old English girl sat patiently as the plane gained altitude. When the signal was given by the pilot, she got in line with the other jumpers.

As she stood in the open doorway, she suddenly saw the image of her dead father. The apparition looked into her eyes and said: "Do not jump again after this."

Pauline was startled as she left the plane and floated safely down to the ground. She gathered her parachute and walked across the grassy field.

She was scheduled to go up later that afternoon, but decided to accept the eerie advice. She told the jumpmaster she had changed her mind about going up, but Pauline watched as the plane taxied out, rolled along the runway and climbed steeply into the sky.

Moments later, the plane rolled over on its back and slammed into the ground. All six people aboard died instantly.

4. WITHOUT A TRACE

"There is a world elsewhere."
—William Shakespeare

Odyssey of the L-8 Blimp

Lieutenant (jg) Ernest D. Cody and Ensign Charles E. Adams were in a cheerful mood that fateful Sunday morning as they manned an L-8 blimp at six o'clock. A grey overcast sky awaited them as they prepared for a routine antisubmarine patrol over San Francisco Bay.

The date was August 16, 1942.

Lieutenant Cody felt the blimp was too heavy with dew to be able to take off. In an attempt to reduce the blimp's weight, he excused a third member of the crew, Machinist's Mate James Hill, from the mission. Hill exited the blimp and returned to the barracks.

Although this patrol, designated Flight 101, was routine for 27-year-old Ernest Cody, it was momentous for Charles Adams. After fifteen years service as a machinist's mate, the 38-year-old sailor had just been commissioned, and this was his first flight as an officer.

Neither man realized it would be his last day on earth.

During the next two hours, Cody and Adams searched for underwater shadows and oil slicks, indicating the possible presence of enemy submarines. Cruising about 300 feet above the water, Cody and Adams waved to crewmen aboard the fishing boats dotting the whitecaps, and noticed a pair of Coast Guard and Navy vessels routinely patrolling the area.

At about 7:50 a.m., Cody spotted an ugly black scar marring the blue water. He alerted the base: "Am investigating suspicious oil slick. Stand by."

Fishermen aboard the small boats saw the blimp drop two smoke flares and feared that it was going to release a depth charge. All eyes were glued to the airship. But the blimp did not drop a bomb or even make another circling pass. The fishermen were astonished to see it soar rapidly upwards and disappear in the overcast.

Operations personnel at Moffett Field had not been able to contact the L-8 since Lieutenant Cody sent his last radio call at 7:50 a.m. They were puzzled, but not alarmed, attributing Cody's silence to radio failure. After all, the weather was clear and both men were airship veterans who could handle an in-flight emergency.

When Cody failed to report at 9:30, Lieutenant Commander George F. Watson, commanding officer of Airship Squadron 32, sent an alert to all ships and aircraft in the area. Surely, someone would see the elusive blimp over San Francisco Bay.

A pair of OS2U Kingfisher airplanes took off from Alameda Naval Air Station to join the search. At 10:20 a Pan American World Airways pilot spotted the airship. Ten minutes later it was seen by one of the Kingfisher pilots, who said it seemed to be out of control. But before he could get close enough to investigate, the L-8 descended into the overcast.

At 10:45 the Army Coast Artillery Station at Fort Funston called Moffett Operations. On a beach near the Olympic Club Lakeside golf course, two surf fishermen had seen the huge blimp coming right at them. They thought her crew must be in trouble, since her two engines had stopped and her propellers were windmilling silently.

When the airship touched down, they had dropped their fishing poles and grabbed her tow lines in a futile effort to ground her. A glance through the gondola's windows revealed nothing amiss—except no one was aboard!

Strong winds had torn the lines from their hands and the blimp danced across the beach until it was blocked by a precipice. One of the depth bombs fell harmlessly to the ground. Then, 300 pounds lighter, the L-8 had risen skyward and vanished over the cliff.

"Any news of the crew?" Watson asked quickly.

"Two men jumped off when she hit the beach," came the answer.

Commander Watson relaxed. At least the crew was safe. Then a puzzling thought: why would Cody and Adams leave the blimp unattended? Both men knew the balloon tradition of "staying with the ship." There was no indication that they had faced grave danger.

A phone call from the police chief in Daly City, a suburb of San Francisco, interrupted his speculation. A blimp had landed on a residential street, severing telephone and electrical wires, colliding with several parked cars and finally coming to rest against a utility pole. A search had failed to find any trace of the crew.

Watson joined the salvage crew at the crash site. A quick inspection revealed that the airship was in excellent condition, though its huge, deflated envelope had been slashed by firemen to see if anyone had been trapped inside.

Then Naval Intelligence presented Watson with a new mystery. After questioning personnel on all the fishing boats, they learned that Cody and Adams had not abandoned the L-8 while it was cruising over the bay, nor had they jumped to the ground when it landed on the beach. Apparently, the Army had mistaken the two surf fishermen for the crew.

Now Watson really began worrying about Cody and Adams. Five hours had passed since their last message. How could they have disappeared from a blimp cruising over a channel crowded with boats?

An extensive search was begun by the Army, Navy, Coast Guard, and state highway patrolmen.

The salvage crew hauled the blimp to a hangar at Moffett, where an examination only deepened the mystery. Her gondola was spotless. Nothing was missing except the bright yellow Mae West life jackets worn by Cody and Adams. All parachutes and the life raft were properly stowed above the polished deck. The radio worked and was set to the proper frequencies. The confidential briefcase was secured. The airship's ignition switches were on and the Warner Super-Scarab engines were operational.

Searchers swept the coastline for weeks, yet no sign of Cody and Adams could be found. What happened to

Lieutenant Cody and Ensign Adams as they circled the bay in view of numerous witnesses?

One investigator suggested that an enemy submarine had surfaced and surprised the blimp. This idea was dismissed, because the sub would have been seen by fishermen as well as the crews of the Coast Guard and Navy vessels.

Another theory proposed that the airmen may have lost their balance and fallen out the door. But the two would have been seen falling into the sea, and their life jackets would have kept them afloat. Besides, the captain of the *Daisy Gray* had seen both men in the L-8 as it cruised over the bay, and the gondola door had been closed.

Regardless of Lieutenant Cody's situation, it is inconceivable that he would not have radioed his problems and intentions to Moffett Field. But, apparently, there was no problem to report. The blimp had suffered no failure of its engines, flight controls, or communications equipment; and all emergency items were intact.

A board of investigation studied volumes of data and interviewed many witnesses. After analyzing the material and testimony, they were no closer to solving the mystery than when they started.

The disappearance of Lieutenant (jg) Ernest Cody and Ensign Charles Adams remains one of the most baffling mysteries of naval aviation.

One of Our Aircraft Is Missing

On a pleasant summer evening in June 1953, Air Defense Command radar picked up an unknown aircraft near Falmouth, Massachusetts. An alert was sounded and a jet fighter scrambled to intercept the target.

The two airmen could not anticipate the bizarre fate awaiting them in the night skies over Cape Cod.

When the klaxon horn began blaring in the ready room at Otis Air Force Base, Captain Suggs and Lieutenant Barkoff rushed to their F-94 Starfire and quickly taxied away from the flight line.

As the all-weather interceptor left the ground, Captain

Suggs retracted the landing gear. Then the unexpected happened. The powerful jet suffered an engine failure. Captain Suggs and Lieutenant Barkoff were moments away from a flaming crash.

"Eject! Eject!" Suggs shouted to his radar officer over the intercom as he jettisoned the canopy.

The Starfire was only six hundred feet above the terrain when Suggs cleared the aircraft. When his parachute blossomed, he did not know if Barkoff had escaped the doomed plane. Suggs looked down, expecting to see the Starfire erupt into a huge broiling ball of orange fire when it crashed. But nothing happened. Everything was serene above and below the confused pilot.

As soon as Suggs' feet hit the ground, he gathered his parachute and stared into the darkness. "Barkoff!" he shouted. "Barkoff, where are you?"

There was no answer from the radar officer.

Suggs had landed in the backyard of a house near the air force base. The owner stepped out of the house and cautiously approached Suggs. "What's going on out here?"

"We just took off when my engine quit," explained Suggs. "We ejected from the plane and I'm looking for my partner. Did you see another parachute?"

"Didn't see nothing," admitted the man. "I was inside till I heard somebody yelling. What happened to your plane?"

"Like I said, the engine failed right after we left the runway at Otis."

"That's not what I mean," said the man. "Where is it? You said you bailed out, but I didn't hear no crash or anything. Sure would have heard something like that, don't you think?"

The man was absolutely right. Suggs' concern for Lieutenant Barkoff had momentarily eclipsed all thoughts of the plane. He glanced into the night sky and realized that something was terribly wrong.

The next morning an extensive search began for the missing plane and radar officer. The tourist season was at its peak and the bay was crowded with cabin cruisers and yachts, as well as commercial fishing boats. Yet no one had seen a crash or heard an explosion.

The conclusion reached by investigators was brief. "A Lockheed F-94C interceptor and one of its crewmen vanished approximately six hundred feet above the ground after the aircraft's engine sustained a flameout immediately after takeoff. No trace of the aircraft or airman has been recovered."

The official analysis of the Starfire incident was apparently correct, but unexplainable. For that reason, the accident report remained classified for several years.

In the Wink of an Eye

The year was 1809. Benjamin Bathurst had already distinguished himself in the foreign service when he was called upon to persuade Austria to join England in opposing Napoleon. In Vienna, he successfully pleaded his case and started back to London.

He almost made it.

When Benjamin Bathurst began his journey home in the fall, he left Berlin with a Prussian passport, an alias, and a package of dispatches, along with his secretary and valet. In Hamburg, a ship was waiting to take them to England.

On November 25, posing as a wealthy merchant named Koch, he stopped in Perleberg for fresh horses, a midday meal, and a rest at the White Swan Inn.

Bathurst went to the local garrison and asked the commanding officer, Captain Klitzing, to post armed guards at the inn to assure his safety. Bathurst was worried that enemy agents would try to steal his dispatch case.

At 9:00 p.m., Bathurst's carriage had a fresh team of horses and he was anxious to get to Lenzen.

While his secretary paid the innkeeper, Bathurst stepped from the building and went towards his coach on the deserted street.

Bathurst walked around his horses—and vanished.

The awestruck witnesses stared in disbelief.

The valet, who was loading baggage, glanced along each side of the coach, but saw only an empty street. The hostler tending the horses could not imagine what had happened to his important passenger. No one saw Bathurst enter the coach, because he disappeared before arriving at its door. The soldiers, standing guard at each end of the narrow street, insisted that no one had passed them.

A search for the 25-year-old Briton was in vain. Captain Klitzing, fearing a severe reprimand, ordered a search of every house in town.

Authorities speculated that Napoleon's agents had kidnapped Bathurst. This inane suggestion was offered in a weak attempt to absolve officials of responsibility for the Englishman's safety.

Nobody could deny one incomprehensible fact.

Benjamin Bathurst had mysteriously vanished on an empty street in a small German town, in full view of four shocked witnesses.

Forty Yards Across the Dunes

On July 24, 1924, two Royal Air Force pilots boarded their single-engine biplane and climbed into the sunny skies over the Mesopotamian desert. Arab hostilities had increased, prompting intelligence officers to schedule daily surveillance flights.

Flight Lieutenant W.T. Day and Pilot Officer D.R. Stewart were flying the morning reconnaissance mission and should have returned in four hours.

The two young men were never seen again.

The operations officer realized something was wrong by the time he dispatched the afternoon reconn sortie.

Where were Day and Stewart?

When the dispatcher calculated that the aircraft had exhausted its fuel supply, it was getting too dark to start looking for the overdue flight.

An aerial search began the following morning and the airplane was found quickly by the rescue team. But a four-day search by air and ground forces found no trace of the two RAF officers. Investigators were stumped, unable to understand why Day and Stewart had landed on the blistering sands.

The airplane was intact and told them a great deal—with the exception of one critical question: what had happened to its crew.

One discovery was bizarre. Day and Stewart had vanished forty yards from their deserted aircraft. That's where their footprints ended in the sand. It looked as if the two airmen had been plucked from the desert by some mysterious force.

Someone suggested that the men had been captured by Arabs, but there were no signs of the struggle that would have taken place if Arabs had attacked the fliers. And the only footprints came from the boots worn by the two airmen.

Meteorologists at the base confirmed that no unusual weather conditions existed that would have prevented Day and Stewart from continuing the flight. Skies were clear and visibility was unlimited.

The abandoned plane had no bullet holes that might have caused the men to make an emergency landing. Investigators could find no oil from the engine streaking along the fuselage. All flight controls worked perfectly and there was sufficient fuel in the tanks. The engine started quickly, and the plane was flown back to the base.

The plane was not the problem. Something else caused the two young men to land on the inhospitable sand dunes.

Flight Lieutenant Day and Pilot Officer Stewart must have seen something in the air or on the sun-bleached desert that made them terminate the flight, climb out of their plane and walk side by side for forty yards. What was it?

5. FINAL VOYAGES

*"For the soul is dead that slumbers,
And things are not what they seem."*
—Henry W. Longfellow

Last Voyage of the *Kamloops*

In the early morning stillness on December 2, 1927, the SS *Kamloops* pulled away from the dock at Cortright, Ontario, and began sailing north along the St. Clair River to Fort William, Ontario, across Lake Superior. She was carrying a cargo of machinery to be delivered to the Thunder Bay Paper Company.

Capt. William Brian was a cautious man, He began to worry about the safety of his valuable freight around noon when he encountered heavy seas. The situation posed no danger to the ship, but could conceivably damage the papermill machinery if it began shifting below decks. He anchored the *Kamloops* until conditions became more favorable.

The weather improved on the afternoon of December 5, and the *Kamloops* again was sailing on course. She approached the *Quedoc,* a steamer commanded by Capt. Roy Simpson.

The two skippers decided to sail together. They were going in the same direction, and it would be easier to estimate the winds and drift.

Something unusual occurred during the next two days that made Brian and Simpson uneasy. On December 7, their calculations indicated that both vessels were far south of their intended course, yet the experienced seamen could find no reason for the navigational error.

Late that afternoon, as the two ships were sailing in tandem, an alert lookout aboard the *Quedoc* noticed a potential danger and reported to Capt. Simpson. Blocking the course ahead at Isle Royale were huge rocks that could slice a fatal gash in a ship's hull. Capt. Simpson reacted quickly.

"Hard a starboard!" he shouted to the helmsman. "Starboard, now!"

Fortunately, the *Quedoc* was able to sail clear of the hazard. Simpson immediately turned his attention to the *Kamloops,* directly behind him. He could not understand why Capt. Brian was not following the *Quedoc* and steering away from the jagged rocks.

Simpson sent a series of short blasts from the steam whistle in an attempt to warn Brian.

Incredibly, the *Kamloops* continued steaming along its original course, oblivious to the *Quedoc's* new heading. Capt. Simpson and his crewmen waved and shouted as the *Kamloops* sailed past them towards the stony formation. They lost sight of it, due to their new course, and proceeded to their destination.

When the *Kamloops'* owners learned she had probably been crushed by rocks along the rugged shoreline at Isle Royale, they sent two company ships to investigate. Hopefully, there would be survivors and the valuable cargo might be recovered if the *Kamloops* were sitting atop the rocks.

The *Midland Prince* and *Islet Prince* steamed across Lake Superior, along with a chartered Canadian tugboat. They were joined by the U.S. Coast Guard cutter *Crawford.*

When the rescue flotilla reached the shores of Isle Royale, they were distressed by what they saw, or rather what they did not see.

There was no sign of the *Kamloops.*

No survivors, no bodies, no life jackets, no wreckage and no cargo. Nothing but jagged rocks peeking ominously above the water.

After passing the *Quedoc,* the *Kamloops* had been certain to hit the rocks. There was no room to maneuver away from the stony hazard. Depending upon the damage sustained, she might have been held in place on the rocky perch, or whipped by heavy waves until her hull collapsed, covering the water and beach with bits and pieces of flotsam.

Search parties combed the beach and a plane was chartered to conduct an aerial survey of the area, but nothing was found.

What had happened to the lost freighter? How could a 2300-ton vessel completely disappear?

The SS *Kamloops* was never seen again.

Wake of the Wicked Clipper

The *Squando* was a jinx even before she slid down the ways in Oslo, Norway. Half a dozen men were killed or injured while building the big clipper ship in 1884.

Before the ship was completed, the widow of a worker who had been killed came to the shipyard and shouted, "I curse this ship and all who sail on her!"

The distraught woman was escorted from the yard and took her own life, along with her unborn child, later that day.

Capt. Nels Erikson, master of the *Squando,* was not superstitious. Not only did he ignore the screaming woman's threats but he also violated a long tradition of the sea by allowing his wife, Selma, to join him for the maiden voyage.

Although the crew felt that it was bad luck to have a woman aboard, their objections fell on deaf ears.

Captain Erikson had started his career as a whaler and this was his first command of a clipper ship. The route would take them across the Atlantic, around Cape Horn, and into the Pacific to San Francisco. But it became clear that the voyage was doomed soon after the majestic ship cleared the harbor in Oslo.

Selma enjoyed evening strolls on the quarterdeck and soon caught the attention of First Mate Lars Gunderson, who began walking with her each night.

Capt. Erikson was a jealous man and became furious upon learning that his wife was socializing with one of his officers. Selma accused Gunderson of stalking her, and offering to kill her husband. Erikson confined Selma to her cabin, and it appeared that his explosive behavior had calmed down.

Just before ending the tormented voyage, however, Capt. Erikson invited the first mate to his quarters. As Gunderson entered the cabin, a bizarre sight awaited him. Selma was trembling in fear as her jealous husband waved a cutlass and shouted wild accusations. As Erikson swung the cutlass, one sweep of the blade cleanly severed the first mate's head.

After the ship docked in San Francisco, the police fished Gunderson's corpse from the bay. They found his head in a wooden bucket under the captain's bunk.

Nels Erikson was found guilty of murder and was hanged.

The *Squando*'s jinx was still in force as she began the long voyage home in November 1884. The new captain was killed when the crew staged a mutiny.

Frightened crewmen often saw a headless sailor pacing the deck during lonely nights at sea.

The third captain slipped and suffered a broken neck in Oslo harbor.

The next skipper became a victim of blood poisoning and died in July, 1885.

Bad luck followed the ship during the next few years as the hapless vessel survived a collision with another ship and ran aground twice.

In 1901, the *Squando* began a journey across the Atlantic, but never reached her destination. She and her crew vanished, and her fate remains one of the great mysteries of the sea.

Cruise to an Unknown Port

When the *Poet* cast off her lines in Philadelphia and steamed into the Atlantic on October 24, 1980, the crew settled in for another mundane voyage to Port Said, Egypt, with a load of grain. Somewhere along the way fate provided a new destination.

The *Poet* never delivered her cargo.

Something unexpected happened to the 12,000-ton freighter shortly after she sailed over the horizon, for she disappeared with all hands.

Normally, Capt. Leroy Warren, master of the *Poet,* maintained daily radio contact with her owners, but no messages were ever received from the vessel.

A massive air-sea search swept the Atlantic, while anxious relatives of the thirty-four crewmen awaited word. Despite a monumental effort to locate the 522-foot freighter, no trace of her or her men was found after six days.

One of the most puzzling aspects of the disappearance was that no other vessels reported seeing the *Poet* along sea lanes crowded with merchant ships. No radio messages were received from the *Poet*'s emergency long-range transmitter, which was designed to activate automatically upon exposure to sea water, and send a continuous distress signal for ten days.

Weather conditions for the *Poet*'s intended course were favorable, according to vessels that should have seen her along the way.

Some people believe the *Poet* became the victim of supernatural forces as yet unknown. Investigators refuse to acknowledge that possibility and believe the freighter's fate has a logical solution. However, the officials have offered no explanation, and the *Poet*'s final port of call remains a mystery.

Ship Without a Crew

In late February 1855, the *James B. Chester* was about six hundred miles southwest of the Azores—an island group about eight hundred miles off the coast of Portugal—when she was spotted by a lookout on the British ship *Marathon.*

Deckhands watched curiously as the three-masted bark sailed closer, her white billowing sails set to keep the big ship sailing on course.

As the *James B. Chester* drew nearer, the British seamen noticed something that caused them to stare in disbelief. There was no helmsman at the wheel. In fact, no crewmen could be seen on deck or in the rigging. The mysterious vessel appeared to be a derelict.

On the *Marathon,* the master's thoughts suddenly

shifted from the bark's unfortunate plight to thoughts of salvage rights.

A boarding party rowed to the strange vessel and made a perplexing discovery. There was no one aboard.

A search above and below decks revealed that some unusual activity had occurred, but there were no signs of violence. Furniture was overturned, articles were scattered in the cabins, drawers ransacked, yet there was no blood nor any indication of the struggle that would have taken place if the vessel had been attacked by pirates or taken over by a rebellious crew.

And, usually, an ill-fated victim of piracy or mutiny was scuttled to remove all evidence that could be used in a maritime court.

A cursory inspection revealed that the cargo was intact, along with the ship's stores and fresh water. All lifeboats were secured in their davits. Only the compass and log book were missing.

The *James B. Chester* had sustained no damage from storms, fires, or explosions.

For some reason, captain and crew had abandoned a vessel that was seaworthy in all respects. This gave rise to a new mystery. How did the crew leave the ship?

The Wayward *Alpena*

On October 16, the *Alpena* was sailing alongside the schooner *Grand Haven*. At high noon the ships parted company five miles from Racine, Wisconsin. If the *Alpena* had been having problems, she could have docked at Racine, yet she continued cruising towards the middle of the lake.

The elegant freight and passenger ship of the Goodrich Line carried nearly a hundred people as she cruised on her southwest course.

Halfway through the passage, at one o'clock in the morning, she met her sister ship, the *Muskegon*. They exchanged whistle salutes as they passed in opposite directions.

Two hours later the *Alpena* was seen by the schooner *Challenger,* about thirty-five miles from Chicago. Everything appeared normal to the *Challenger*'s crew. At this time of the morning, however, the *Alpena* should have already reached Chicago.

Other curious events occurred for which no explanations have been found.

Aboard the *S. A. Irish,* a barge being towed to Milwaukee, the crew watched in bewilderment as the *Alpena* followed them for three hours. By now the passenger ship was far north of her normal course.

On October 16, the *Alpena* was sailing alongside the schooner, *Grand Haven.* At high noon the ships parted company five miles from Racine, Wisconsin. If the *Alpena* had been having problems, she could have docked at Racine, yet she continued cruising towards the middle of the lake.

That afternoon the schooner *Levi Grant* came within one and a half miles of the *Alpena.* Crewmen aboard the schooner noted that her wheels were turning and the steam whistle was squealing. All appeared normal.

However, a few things were not normal.

Although steam was seen coming from the *Alpena*'s engines, no smoke was flowing from her stacks. Then, suddenly, as the crewmen on the *Levi Grant* watched, the *Alpena* vanished.

One moment she was in sight, and then she ceased to exist. Obviously, a large sailing vessel cannot sink in the time it takes to blink an eye. So, what could have happened? The mystery of the *Alpena* was never solved. But it was not an isolated case. Witnesses saw the same thing happen to the *Bannockburn* twelve years later.

Gone—Temporarily

On November 21, 1902, the *Bannockburn* was hauling grain across Lake Superior. Sailing towards the large steel ship was the *Algonquin,* commanded by Capt. James McMaugh.

As the two vessels approached each other, McMaugh thought the British-built *Bannockburn* was a work of art and asked the mate for his opinion of the elegant ship.

When the mate looked out the windows, all he saw was an empty horizon. "What ship are you talking about, Captain?"

McMaugh looked again, but the *Bannockburn* had vanished. Where had she gone? What force could cause such a huge ship to disappear so swiftly?

Theories to explain such disappearances are as numerous as the events themselves.

Some people believe that certain areas of the world generate an electromagnetic anomaly, which creates vortices that can transport material objects within the Space-Time continuum. This could account for ships that vanish instantaneously. It might be possible for them to reappear in other time periods or in a dimension as yet unknown. Some vessels have become legendary for their ability to slip in and out of sight. Among these ghost ships are the *Flying Dutchman,* a legendary schooner spotted by sailors during the last four hundred years near the Cape of Good Hope.

Another vessel that appears to anxious seamen is the *Kobenhavn,* which was the largest ship in the world when it vanished after sailing from Buenos Aires with a full complement of Danish naval cadets on December 14, 1928. Although equipped with radios, no distress signal was ever heard and she disappeared with all hands. The following year, sailors reported sighting a ship answering the *Kobenhavn*'s description near Easter Island in the Pacific. The phantom ship was next seen by passengers on a liner bound for Panama. Seamen have reported seeing the ghostly *Kobenhavn* as late as 1961, while cruising among the Solomon Islands.

And the majestic *Bannockburn* has been seen many times over the years since she vanished on Lake Superior in 1902.

6. FLIGHTS INTO OBLIVION

*"Nothing is so firmly believed
as what we least know."*
—Montaigne

A Beautiful Day for Flying

The sunny skies offered a light easterly breeze as Andrew Carnegie Whitfield climbed into his silver and red monoplane at noon on April 15, 1938. Moments later the craft began rolling along the turf runway and was soon airborne.

Whitfield's airplane carried ten gallons of gas, which would allow him to fly for as long as three hours. He had told friends he was going to Brentwood and would return before sunset.

Andrew Whitfield, a nephew of billionaire philanthropist Andrew Carnegie, was proud of his private pilot's license. He had logged two hundred hours, and was only fifty hours away from taking his flight test for a commercial license.

The twenty-eight-year-old Princeton graduate loved flying, but never expressed any thoughts of becoming a professional aviator. He was content to "slip the surly bonds of earth" just for the fun of it.

Whitfield departed from Roosevelt Field on the same runway Charles Lindbergh used on his historic transatlantic flight. But Whitfield's destination was only twenty-two miles away across dry land.

Andrew Whitfield should have arrived at Brentwood Airport around twelve-thirty, but he never landed there . . . or anywhere else.

An extensive five-day air and ground search yielded no clues. Scores of people combed every field where the missing flier might have made an emergency landing.

It seemed impossible that Whitfield's plane could vanish over a densely populated area. Yet, that's exactly what happened one sunny afternoon during a thirty-minute flight over Long Island.

No one ever saw Andrew Whitfield again.

Déjà Vu over the Sierra Madre

On the morning of December 19, 1979, three jet fighters of the Singapore Air Force departed Clark Air Base on a routine training mission. The eager pilots were anxious to prove they had the right stuff to hit the bull's-eye on the targets.

They never arrived at the bombing area.

After taking off at 10:40, the pilots were in constant radio contact with air traffic control as they flew towards the Crow Valley Bombing Range, only twenty miles from the airfield.

The three A4 Skyhawks were fast, highly maneuverable, single-engine interceptors, built by Douglas Aircraft in California.

Radar operators tracked the Skyhawks as they cruised above the Sierra Madre mountains.

Suddenly the three fighter planes disappeared simultaneously from the radar screens. Astonished operators quickly tried to contact the pilots but received no response.

The operations officer thought the planes had collided and launched a rescue helicopter in hopes that the fliers had been able to eject.

As the helicopter flew towards the last known position of the doomed trio, the aircrew looked for the fire and smoke that would pinpoint the crash site.

Initial reports from the rescue team were negative. No wreckage or parachutes had been seen.

If the Skyhawks had been flying over water, the rescuers might have been able to rationalize their failure to find the debris from a crash. But after two days of dawn-to-dusk searches, they could not explain why no wreckage was found from three airplanes flying over land.

Whatever happened must have taken place with such swiftness that no distress call could be sent by the ill-fated airmen.

Ironically, this was not the first time airplanes from Clark Air Base had mysteriously disappeared over the Sierra Madre mountain range.

Five years earlier, four Philippine Air Force jets vanished without a trace while flying the same route as the three Singapore planes.

Lost over the English Channel

On a cold, rainy afternoon near Bedford, England, a small airplane took off and climbed into an overcast sky en route to Paris. The single-engine plane's two passengers were an Army colonel and a musician. Moments later the plane slipped into the clouds.

It was never seen again.

When news of Glenn Miller's disappearance hit the papers, it momentarily stilled the hearts of all people who loved popular music. One of the world's most successful bandleaders had become another victim of World War Two, which had already taken so many soldiers who had marched away to the sound of his music.

It was in Passaic, New Jersey, in 1942, that Glenn Miller announced he was disbanding his orchestra and joining the Army. Many fans, and others in the music business, believe this decision marked the beginning of the end for big bands.

On December 4, 1942, the ex-civilian became Captain Glenn Miller and launched plans to modernize military music for the Army Air Force.

The idea was not music to the ears of his superior officers. Miller was soon running a challenging obstacle course, designed by conservative, tone-deaf generals opposed to change. After more than a year of heated confrontations, the Army brass surrendered reluctantly.

In 1943 Miller's innovative military band was heard on a weekly radio show throughout the CBS network, and it also recorded programs that were sent to the troops. Miller's most ambitious project was to take the band to Europe to entertain servicemen with special concerts, but the top brass erected another obstacle course.

Eventually, after nearly a year of badgering the War Department, Miller received orders to take his band to England in June, 1944.

During the next five and a half months, Glenn Miller's modern Army Air Force band thrilled thousands of servicemen at seventy-one concerts.

Miller was promoted to major on August 17, 1944, and began planning a Christmas concert for the troops in Paris.

Miller was scheduled to fly to Paris on December 14, but bad weather postponed the flight. He received a call from Colonel Norman Baesell, who was flying there the next day in the general's personal plane. Baesell invited Miller to join him.

That night Miller had dinner with his executive officer, Lieutenant Don Haynes, at the Officers' Club in Bedford, England. Haynes had been Miller's personal manager in civilian life, and the two men spent the evening discussing plans for a postwar band.

The weather was still dreary the next morning, but the forecast called for clearing in the afternoon. Miller and Haynes spent the morning eating breakfast and reading the newspaper. Then they drove to Twinwood Farm, fifty miles northwest of London. The plane was en route from another air station.

Miller was uneasy about flying and appeared very nervous as they waited in the staff car. The rain had become a steady drizzle, and he wondered if the pilot would be able to find them beneath the thick overcast.

Suddenly they heard a plane. The ceiling was about two hundred feet with poor visibility, but Flight Officer John Morgan was an experienced instrument pilot. The single-engine Norseman broke through the overcast, circled the field, and landed a few minutes later. Morgan taxied to the car, swung around and kept the engine running.

Miller and Baesell tossed their baggage into the plane and then climbed aboard. While buckling their seat belts, Miller said, "Hey, where are the parachutes?"

"What's the matter, Miller?" said Baesell. "Do you want to live forever?"

At 1:55 p.m., Flight Officer Morgan released the brakes, began moving rapidly down the runway and was soon airborne. Less than a minute later the Norseman was swallowed by clouds.

Surprisingly, Glenn Miller's plane was not reported missing until Christmas Eve, nine days after it vanished.

Army officials believe the Norseman had been disabled by ice and crashed into the English Channel.

Others disagree, and believe Miller's plane may have gone down over land. One who shares the latter theory is Dixie Clark, a radio operator at Twinwood Farm.

Shortly after takeoff, Flight Officer Morgan failed to respond to radio transmissions. Dixie Clark called several times, but got no answer. She is certain the plane never made it to the Channel.

Glenn Miller had many friends and fans who were upset by the Army's apparent indifference to his disappearance. They could not understand why a full-scale search was not launched when his plane did not land in Paris.

One reason was the Battle of the Bulge, a vital military operation that began on December 15—one day after Miller left England. Authorities were concentrating on blocking Germany's last major advance through the Ardennes Mountains in Belgium. They were not concerned about one overdue airplane when planes failed to return every day during the war. There wasn't time to search for them. Pilots and planes were desperately needed for combat, and could not be spared for rescue missions.

An unusual incident occurred two days after Miller departed for Paris. Military policemen went to the Mount Royal Hotel, collected all of his belongings and drove away. Allen Stillwell, Miller's personal valet, thought this was very odd since his boss had not yet been officially declared dead or missing. When Stillwell asked why the items were being boxed, the men said everything was being sent to his family. But his family never received any of Miller's clothes or personal effects.

The C64 Norseman that took Glenn Miller to an unknown destination was capable of making the flight that fateful Friday afternoon. The single-engine transport, used as a cargo and passenger plane during the war, could carry nine people at one hundred forty-eight miles per hour. It had no de-icing equipment, however, and many theorists believe that caused it to crash into the English Channel. Meteorologists, however, said icing conditions did not exist before or after the plane departed Twinwood Farm.

Flight Officer Morgan, a veteran of thirty-two combat missions in B-24 bombers, had spent one hour flying on instruments in thick clouds before picking up Miller and Baesell. He would never have flown a small plane anywhere that day if the weathermen had forecast icing at any altitude along his route to Twinwood Farm or Paris.

Icing is not the sole culprit responsible for aircraft disasters, yet it was the Army's only explanation for the doomed plane. Investigators never considered engine failure a probable cause.

If the Norseman had crashed before reaching the Channel, it seems likely that someone would have found it by now. During the Battle of Britain, the rugged hills and farmlands became a graveyard for scores of Allied and Axis aircraft. Since the war, an army of collectors daily roam the sites looking for wrecks and artifacts.

The fate of Glenn Miller may never be known, yet the famous bandleader may have unwittingly predicted his epitaph a few weeks before his final journey.

In a letter to his brother, Miller said, "By the time you receive this, we shall all be in Paris, barring of course a nose-dive into the Channel."

Flight 11 Is Missing— *Again*

On August 15, 1976, Flight 11 taxied away from the Saeta Airlines gate in Quito, Equador, and took off for a short journey to Cuenca. When the airliner was eight minutes away from its destination, the captain called the tower with his position and was cleared to land.

Flight 11 never arrived.

Extensive searches failed to find any trace of the four-engine Vickers Viscount and its fifty-nine passengers.

The airline's president said, "It's possible the aircraft may have crashed, but it was only eight minutes away from Cuenca. And it's not possible to crash that close without detection."

Then, nearly three years later, it happened again. Another Saeta Viscount, also designated Flight 11, departed Quito on April 23, 1979. The crew made a routine report to the Ambato Relay Station, and then vanished with fifty-seven passengers.

After each airliner disappeared, massive air and land searches were made by army patrols, and planes from the Ecuadorean and American air forces.

In both incidents weather conditions were excellent and each plane had been in contact with the Ambato Relay Station. During the flight involving the second Viscount, the captain was called on the company frequency by another plane that requested a weather report. Capt. Eduin Alexandre said, "The sky is beautiful and everything's fine."

Those were his last words.

If either Viscount had experienced an in-flight emergency, one of the pilots could have called the Ambato Relay Station. Whatever happened must have occurred so swiftly that neither crew had time to report the problem.

Investigators admitted they could not explain how two large turboprop airliners could vanish over land on a forty-five-minute flight in good weather.

Although a substantial reward was offered by the Ecuadorean government, Saeta Airlines, and grieving families, the fate of the one hundred sixteen passengers has never been determined.

7. PHANTOM WARRIORS

*"The muffled drum's sad roll has beat
The soldier's last tatoo."*
—Theodore O'Hara

In the Midnight Hour

In April 1945, Allied forces in Europe were on the threshold of victory. Germany's generals had lost hope the previous summer, when Eisenhower's troops captured the beaches at Normandy.

Adolf Hitler committed suicide on April 30, and the war ended eight days later.

A few weeks earlier, an American infantry unit had taken Amasdorf, a sheep village on the west bank of the Elbe River. Lieutenant Al van Detta set up headquarters in one of the buildings and awaited further orders.

One morning Privates Jay F. Rivera and Richard O'Leary found their names on the list for sentry duty. At midnight they reported to their post and began their lonely task. Although only nineteen years old, the two combat veterans were used to a lot more action than guarding a grove of trees at the edge of town.

Thirty minutes later, O'Leary could no longer tolerate the boredom. "I'm going to get some coffee, Jay. I'll be right back."

It was a serious offense to leave your post, but Rivera knew he could handle the job alone. He settled down again and stared across the moonless terrain, wondering if any of the Führer's master race were lurking in the shrubbery.

About ten minutes later, Rivera heard someone approaching from behind. He turned around, expecting to see O'Leary, and was surprised to see Private Michael Prettyboy, a friend from another platoon.

"Hello, Michael," said Rivera. "What are you doing out here?"

"I couldn't sleep and decided to take a walk," answered Prettyboy. "How come you're alone on guard duty?"

"Oh, I'm not," said Rivera. "O'Leary's with me but he went to get some coffee. He'll be back soon."

The two friends talked about the war and told each other of their experiences during the past week.

Prettyboy then got up and grabbed his rifle. "I'll see you later, Jay. I've got guard duty myself in another hour."

O'Leary soon returned and the two boys remained at the isolated outpost until relieved at two o'clock.

Six hours later, Rivera was eating breakfast and overheard others talking about gunfire during the night. Apparently, a sentry had fired at someone in the open field.

"You know," said Rivera. "It could have been Michael Prettyboy out there last night. He came across the field to see me when I was on guard duty."

Lieutenant van Detta stopped sipping coffee and looked suspiciously at Rivera. "Are you sure about that?"

"Yes, sir," said Rivera. "You can ask O'Leary."

"That won't be necessary," said van Detta.

Suddenly, Rivera felt uneasy and wondered if the platoon leader knew about O'Leary leaving his post the night before. Perhaps the lieutenant was trying to get him to confirm O'Leary's absence.

"Sir," pleaded Rivera, "I'm sure O'Leary will remember. Just ask him."

"I don't have to," said van Detta. "If you and O'Leary saw Prettyboy last night, you were either dreaming or drunk on duty. Private Prettyboy was killed in action yesterday morning."

Duty, Honor, and Valor

In 1885 Geronimo went on a deadly spree of looting and murder throughout the Southwest. Scores of U.S. Cavalry troops vainly tried to halt the Apaches, who left in their wake an appalling number of dead and mutilated settlers. But the Indian warriors moved like the wind and eluded General George Crook's soldiers.

Geronimo's rampaging Indians fled into Mexico to escape confrontation with Crook's troopers, who quickly began scouting the border.

In Mexico, Major Carlos Fernandez was sure that the Indians would attempt to find a way back into Arizona. He and his twelve troopers had been chasing a band of Apaches towards the border for eight days. The major was a highly experienced combat veteran who had been awarded several medals for leadership under fire.

Major Fernandez led his weary soldiers close to an Apache camp where he and a private went on a scouting mission. They ran into a small group of Indians and the private was killed in the ensuing battle. Fernandez made it back to his men, who wondered how their leader had managed to escape. His tattered uniform was bloody and a thin line of crimson liquid trickled down under his dusty cap.

Fernandez had clearly received a dangerous head wound but he refused all attempts to be treated. He waved his men away and pulled the cap down to his eyelashes.

The Indians attacked that afternoon and the battle continued until sundown. At dawn both sides were again firing and continued until the Apaches abandoned the battleground. Remarkably, none of the soldiers had died during the exhausting conflict.

Major Fernandez assembled his men and rode into the nearest town. He sat tall in the saddle for a moment, said, "Thank God, my work is done," and then fell to the ground.

The sergeant ran to his commander and checked for a pulse, but found none. As the soldiers gathered around their fallen leader, the sergeant removed the major's cap. They gasped and made the sign of the cross upon their chests when they saw a blood-encrusted bullet hole in the major's forehead—a mortal wound he had received while scouting the Apache camp.

During the past two days, as the valiant soldiers held off a force nearly three times greater than they had anticipated, they had been led by a dead man.

Against All Odds

On the afternoon of April 16, 1951, the HMS *Affray* slipped away from the dock and sailed from Portsmouth. The British submarine was on a routine training cruise and informed her base she was beginning her dive at 9:15 p.m.

It was the last message she would send.

The communications staff at Portsmouth became worried when the *Affray* failed to make any additional reports.

On April 17, the Admiralty initiated search operations on a massive scale. All attempts to signal the sub by radio were answered with silence as the search armada crisscrossed thousands of square miles off the English and French coastlines.

When no trace was found of the submarine and her

seventy-five crewmen after two days, search operations were suspended.

The job of finding *Affray*'s watery grave fell to HMS *Reclaim,* a salvage vessel that would investigate a wide expanse of ocean, scattered with more than two hundred sunken ships. Fortunately, time and manpower could be saved during the arduous task by using underwater television cameras attached to the hull of the salvage ship.

After scanning the sea bottom for two months, the weary crewmen of the *Reclaim* were ready to give up. The submarine could not be located among the sunken vessels within the search grid. Many sailors felt the chances of finding the elusive *Affray* were a million to one.

Meanwhile, the wife of a British admiral was getting ready for bed one night when she suddenly felt she was not alone. She turned and was startled to see a naval officer near the door. She recognized the man at once, for he had often been a guest in their home while serving with her husband during the war. He stood very still, his eyes staring vacantly, and she was confused by his sorrowful expression.

"Tell your husband we are at the north end of Hurd Deep, nearly seventy miles from the lighthouse at Saint Catherine's Point," said the officer. "It happened very suddenly and none of us expected it."

Before she could speak, the man disappeared.

After recovering her composure she called her husband, who was then logging time at a desk. She told him of the mysterious visit from their friend.

After the admiral passed the officer's mystical message to the Admiralty, the HMS *Reclaim* quickly weighed anchor and sailed to the new search area.

On June 14, as television cameras under the salvage ship were scanning a wreck on the outskirts of Hurd Deep, the operator spotted a nameplate belonging to the missing submarine. Her hull lay peacefully on the seabed where she came to rest forty miles from her diving point. The doomed submarine was never raised, so the cause of her distress was never determined.

One fact was certain. HMS *Affray*'s last resting place would still be unknown if the admiral's wife had not been told its true position by one of her officers, who came to visit their home one last time.

And Then There Were None

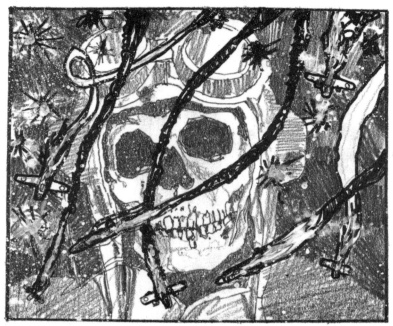

The Battle of Britain had just ended, and the Royal Air Force had won a momentary victory in the skies over London in the fall of 1940. The myth of the Luftwaffe's supremacy had been shattered as Germany's elite fighter squadrons retreated to consider their losses.

Although Britain's aerial triumph was only temporary, it gave Bomber Command time to attack German military installations along the occupied eastern coasts of the English Channel. These targets were heavily defended, but they had to be destroyed before the Luftwaffe had a chance to regroup.

One RAF squadron was selected to attack the critical

German targets with tactics that were bold and extremely dangerous. The bombers would go in low, drop their bombs and get away as fast as their twin-engine planes could fly. The mission was so important that Bomber Command sent an air marshal to oversee the mission. He would debrief the aircrews upon their return and forward the information to headquarters.

Twelve A-20 Havoc medium bombers started their engines, taxied to the runway and were soon airborne. The planes were American-built and each carried a pilot, copilot, bombardier, and a two-thousand-pound bomb load.

Now came the worst part of the mission for those left behind—the waiting. As the sun began to slide below the horizon, the air marshal drank tea and calculated the time when he could expect the planes to return.

Hours later, he heard the distant drone of aircraft engines and went outside. He looked up at the sky as he walked to the Operations building, but it was too dark to see the approaching planes.

The air marshal wondered how many crews had returned as the planes taxied to the parking area and shut down their engines. A few minutes later, he heard the sound of vehicles stopping outside; then nine weary airmen came into the room. Their haggard expressions revealed the terrible ordeal they had survived.

"At ease, men," said the air marshal. "I know you've seen a lot of sky today and I won't keep you longer than necessary." He paused, then realized he was looking at only three crews. Where were the men from the remaining nine bombers? "Did any more planes make it back?"

The weary airmen shook their heads, and one of the pilots described the furious antiaircraft fire and flak that had covered the sky like a black blanket. He said the low-level bomb run had been successful, but very costly. The only planes to survive were in the first wave. By the time the remaining bombers started their run, the German gunners had pinpointed the range and shot the planes to pieces.

Nine planes out of twelve had been lost, along with twenty-seven men. It had been a catastrophe, and the air marshal found it difficult to believe that any planes had survived. The crewmen completed their written reports and signed their names.

"Well done, boys," said the air marshal. "You deserve a well-earned drink and a good night's rest. The bar is open."

The airmen departed and left the marshal to agonize over the fact that seventy-five percent of the attacking force had been destroyed during a single mission. Headquarters was not going to be satisfied with the disastrous news.

The air marshal's gloomy thoughts were interrupted by his aide, who walked to the table and sat down. "I don't quite know how to say this, sir, but we had some tremendous losses today."

"I know," the air marshal said and sighed. "We lost nine planes."

The aide looked puzzled. "No, sir, you've got the wrong number."

The air marshal's eyes reflected a flicker of hope. "Did some of the planes land somewhere else? That's good news."

"Sir, I don't understand what you mean. We lost all of the planes on today's mission."

"You're mistaken," argued the marshal. "Three made it back here. I just debriefed the crews and sent them to the bar for a nightcap."

The aide stared at his superior in disbelief. "I don't know what you're talking about, sir. All of the bombers were shot down over the target."

The air marshal rose, took the written reports from his folder and tossed them on the table. "Then how do you explain these? I watched the men fill those out and sign them."

The aide stared at the documents and noticed that the names, ranks and aircraft numbers were the same as three of the crews listed as killed in action that day.

"Are you telling me the men I debriefed are dead? Look at the dates and times."

"I'm sorry, sir," said the aide. "I can't explain it. But none of the planes landed here and the bar has been empty all night."

Confirmation came the next day. All twelve bombers had been shot down by German antiaircraft fire. There were no survivors. Another startling fact was discovered when the official results of the bombing attack arrived. The information contained in the reports made by the dead crewmen precisely matched the actual damage to the target.

Nine men had filled out the papers and signed their names. Nine men, who had died hours before they described the horrors of that tragic afternoon to the air marshal, had then walked out of the room and were never seen again.

About the Author

Ron Edwards was raised in California and Hawaii, and holds a B.A. in journalism from Columbia Pacific University. After a tour of duty with the U.S. Air Force, assigned to the North American Air Defense Command in Colorado Springs, Colorado, he became a radio broadcaster and television writer. His feature articles on aviation, space and military history have appeared in numerous national magazines. After fourteen years in broadcasting, he changed careers and spent the next ten years as a pilot for a regional airline. He is now a full-time writer and lives in Phoenix, Arizona.

About the Illustrator

Born in Vernon, Texas, Jim Sharpe attended Texas Tech before becoming a carrier jet pilot in the Navy. He later worked in Detroit as an art director, illustrator, and designer, and in 1968 began his freelance career. His work includes many covers for *Time, TV Guide, Newsweek,* and others, illustrations for many magazines and books, and special commissions from government offices (including many postage stamps, and five coins for the U.S. Mint), Lincoln Center, the Kennedy Center, and PBS ("The Civil War"). Jim now lives and works in Denton, Texas.

Index